Stars

KER THAN

Children's Press®
A Division of Scholastic Inc.
New York Toronto London Auckland Sydney
Mexico City New Delhi Hong Kong
Danbury, Connecticut

Content Consultant

Noreen Grice

Astronomer

President, You Can Do Astronomy, LLC.

www.youcandoastronomy.com

Library of Congress Cataloging-in-Publication Data

Than, Ker, 1980-
  Stars / by Ker Than.
     p. cm.—(A true book)
  Includes index.
     ISBN 13: 978-0-531-16899-8 (lib. bdg.)   978-0-531-22806-7 (pbk.)
     ISBN 10: 0-531-16899-9 (lib. bdg.)   0-531-22806-1 (pbk.)

1. Stars—Juvenile literature. I. Title. II. Series.

QB801.7.T45 2010
523.8—dc22   2008051630

1 2 3 4 5 6 7 8 9 10 R 19 18 17 16 15 14 13 12 11 10   62

Find the Truth!

Everything you are about to read is true *except* for one of the sentences on this page.

Which one is **TRUE**?

T or F Stars live forever and never change at all.

T or F Stars are made from clouds of gas and dust called nebulae.

Find the answers in this book.

Nebula

3

Contents

Chandra X-ray Observatory

A star's twinkling is caused by gases moving in Earth's atmosphere.

THE BIG TRUTH!

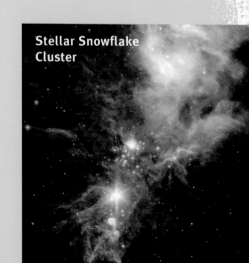

Stellar Snowflake Cluster

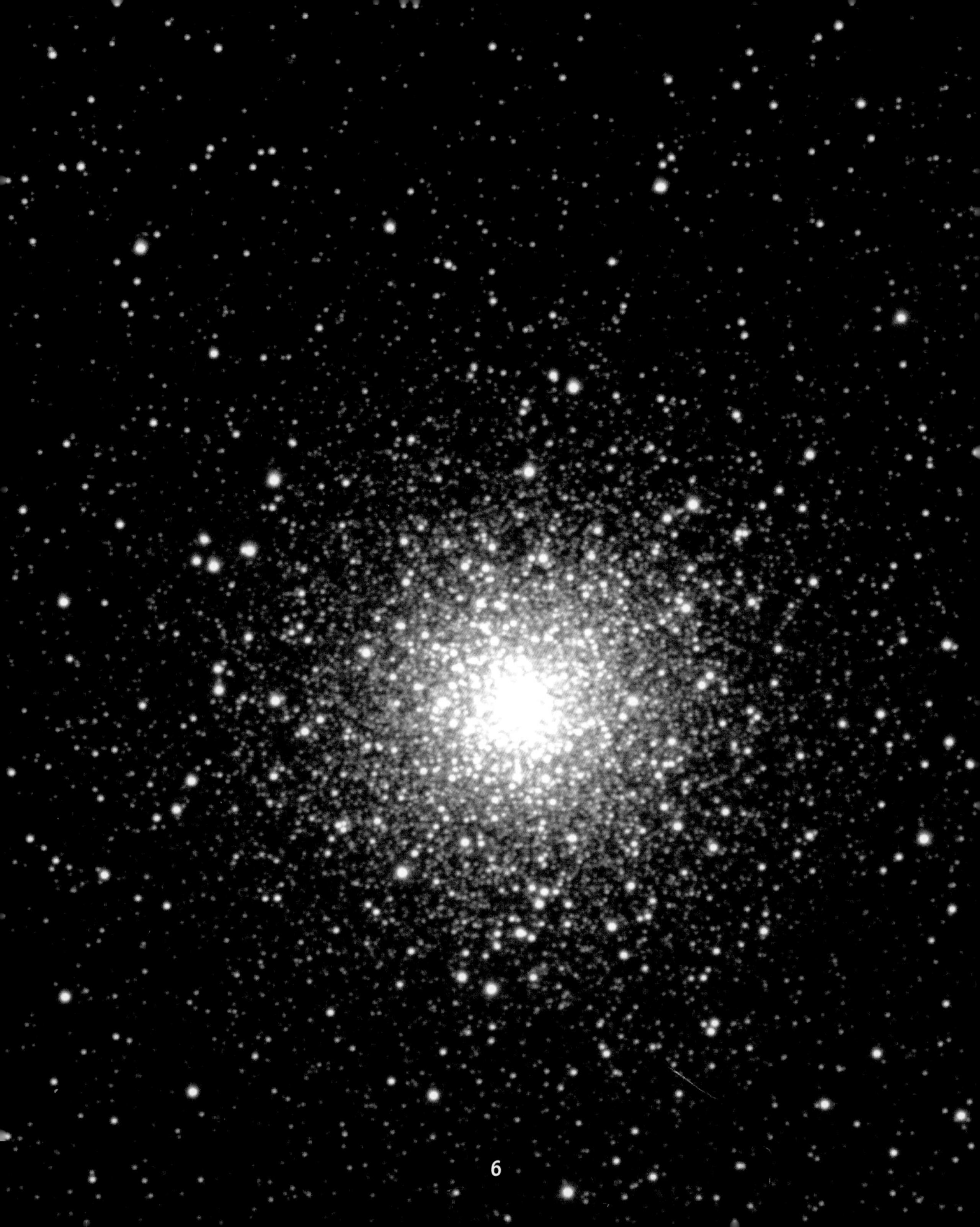

CHAPTER 1

Thank the Stars

When the universe first formed billions of years ago, there were no stars, planets, or moons. But now, about 14 billion years later, the universe is a different place. Today, scientists know that there are billions of trillions of such objects in space.

The oldest known stars are about 13 billion years old.

The Stars and You

A starry night is a beautiful sight, but there is more to stars than just the light you see. Stars are big balls of glowing gas and, like people, they have a special life cycle. Stars are born, grow old, and die. The gases from old stars flow into space to help make newer stars, like our Sun. All of the basic elements that are found in animals and plants on Earth, like carbon and iron, may have been created inside the centers of stars. And, like people, no two stars are exactly the same.

The Sun is the closest star to Earth.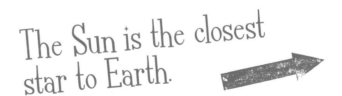

The Sun is 93 million miles
(150 million kilometers) away from Earth.

9

The bright stars in the center of the Rosette Nebula are a few million years old.

CHAPTER 2

A Star Is Born

Besides stars and planets, space is filled with giant clouds of gas and dust. These clouds are called **nebulae** (NEH-byoo-lee). Nebulae are mostly made of hydrogen gas. These huge clouds are where a star's life begins in the universe. A single nebula may have enough gas and dust to form hundreds or thousands of stars.

Nebulae are gigantic—they can be trillions of miles wide.

Protostars

Over hundreds of thousands of years, **gravity** slowly causes gas and dust in a nebula to clump together and spin around. Gravity is the invisible force that pulls two objects toward each other. As the cloud spins, it gets hotter and thicker. Finally, the gas and dust get so thick that they collapse into a ball called a **protostar**. Dust and gas are crushed together in the core, or center, of the protostar. This makes the core heat up.

A protostar can be seen forming inside this cloud of gas and dust.

If Jupiter were 80 times more massive, it would have become a star.

After the core reaches a temperature of several millions of degrees, it begins to use hydrogen as fuel. A star's fire isn't the same kind made by burning wood or coal. This kind of fire is called **nuclear fusion** (NOO-klee-ur FYOO-zhuhn). When a protostar's core begins to burn this way, it becomes a star.

The Eagle Nebula

In 1995, the Hubble Space Telescope snapped this photo of the giant gas and dust clouds in the Eagle Nebula. The clouds were nicknamed the "Pillars of Creation." Scientists think our Sun was born in a gas and dust cloud like this one. Many newborn stars have formed in these pillars.

Newborn stars can be seen forming in the nebula.

Thousands of stars in this starburst cluster in NGC 3603 are more massive than our Sun.

 Scientists guess that there are billions of galaxies in the universe.

Clusters and Galaxies

Many stars can form from one nebula. Stars are often born together in pairs called binary stars and groups called **star clusters**. A star cluster can have hundreds or thousands of stars that were all born at around the same time. The largest groups of stars, with billions of members, are called **galaxies**.

The two huge Keck telescopes in
Hawaii can work together to provide
the clearest views of stars.

CHAPTER 3

All Grown Up

All stars spend most of their lives burning hydrogen. Some stars are smaller than our Sun, while others are hundreds of times larger than it. There are white stars, red stars, blue stars, and yellow stars like our Sun. Some stars give off a lot of light, while others hardly give off any at all.

Scientists think that most stars in the universe give off less light than the Sun.

Size and Color

Scientists group stars by their size and temperature. Stars that are the same size as our Sun or smaller are called **dwarfs**. Stars that are tens of times larger than our Sun are called **giants**. Stars that are hundreds of times larger than our Sun are called **supergiants**.

Comparison of Star Sizes

The temperature on the surface of a star also affects the color of its light. The hottest stars look blue. The coolest stars appear red. Stars can also be yellow, white, and orange. The temperature on the surface of a yellow dwarf like our Sun is about 10,000°F (5,500°C). A red dwarf is only about half as hot. The surface of a blue giant can be 10 times hotter!

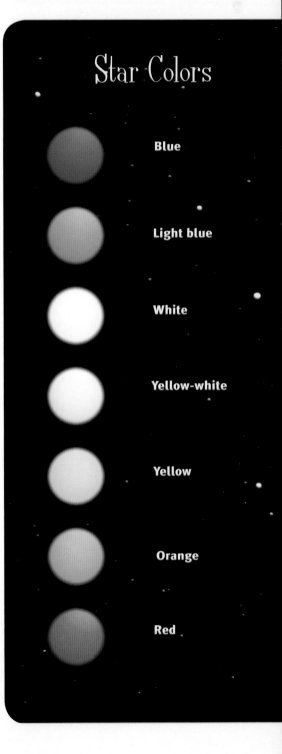

Star Colors

Blue

Light blue

White

Yellow-white

Yellow

Orange

Red

The Helix Nebula surrounds a white dwarf
that is slowly fading and dying.

CHAPTER 4

Burning Out

Eventually, all stars run out of the gases they need. After the hydrogen in a star's core begins to run out, different things can happen. Small and medium-sized stars, like our Sun, lose their outer layers, while their cores slowly fade and die out. Very large stars can end their lives in gigantic explosions.

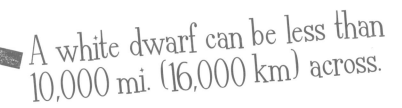

A white dwarf can be less than 10,000 mi. (16,000 km) across.

Star Changes

As a star slowly runs out of fuel in its core, the core shrinks and heats up. Its high temperature causes the rest of the star to expand like a balloon. But the outer layers of the star are much cooler, so the star glows red and becomes a red giant. While the dying star continues to burn, its outer layers drift away into space. After a few million years, the outer layers are completely gone. The star is now much smaller. When the star finally runs out of fuel in its core, the fire goes out.

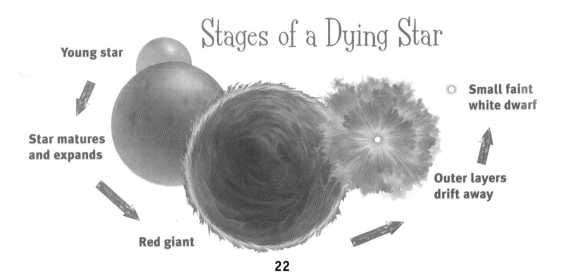

Stages of a Dying Star

Young star

Star matures
and expands

Red giant

Outer layers
drift away

Small faint
white dwarf

White dwarf

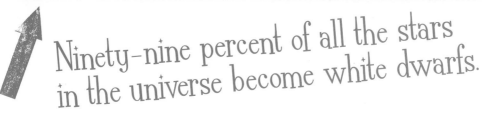

Ninety-nine percent of all the stars in the universe become white dwarfs.

The star is now a white dwarf. Although there is no more nuclear fusion, the white dwarf is hot enough to glow white. White dwarfs cool down slowly over time. After billions of years, they become dark and cold. Cold stars like these are called black dwarfs.

Life of a Large Star

Small and medium-sized stars can burn for a very long time—up to trillions of years! But very large stars don't live as long. They only give off energy for a few million years. That's because the cores of large stars have much higher temperatures and use up their fuel faster. Once a very large star runs out of energy, its core collapses because of gravity. When some very large stars collapse, they can cause a powerful explosion called a **supernova**.

Scientists think that a star explodes every 50 years in our galaxy, the Milky Way.

In 1987, scientists discovered a supernova explosion in a nearby galaxy and named it SN 1987A.

Supernovae

A star takes millions of years to form. But it only takes days for a star to explode into a supernova. At its brightest, a supernova outshines whole galaxies. A supernova flings all the dust and gases from its outer layers into space. These star "leftovers" become the building blocks for more stars and planets. Many materials found on Earth, like carbon and iron, probably came from distant stars.

SN 1987A

SN 1987A was a supernova that first appeared in 1987. It was caused by a blue supergiant star in a nearby galaxy. Like other supernovae, scientists found SN 1987A when the light from the explosion reached us on Earth. In this case, that was 170,000 years after the event!

Bright Star

In 1054 C.E., Chinese skywatchers reported spotting a star that was so bright, it could be seen in the daytime. It slowly faded from view and astronomers later discovered the Crab Nebula, where the bright star had been seen.

Life After a Supernova

If a star's core survives a supernova, one of two things can happen. A star that is four to eight times the size of our Sun shrinks. It collapses into a tiny **neutron star** only a few miles wide. Even though it's small, a neutron star is very heavy. A spoonful of it would weigh about a billion tons (900,000,000 metric tons) on Earth. That's as much as a mountain!

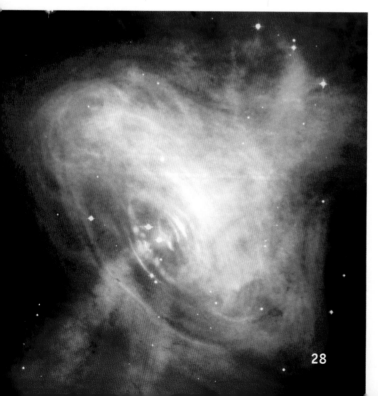

This picture shows the heart of the Crab Nebula. It is where the leftover core of the star from the supernova seen in 1054 C.E. is found.

Scientists believe there's a supermassive black hole in the center of our Milky Way Galaxy.

Instead of collapsing into a neutron star, the core of a supernova can sometimes turn into a **black hole**. The center of a black hole is much smaller than the period at the end of a sentence. But at the same time, it's heavier than a neutron star. A black hole's gravity is so strong that nothing can escape it—not even light.

A Star's Life

Over billions of years, a star's life has many stages.

Small/medium star

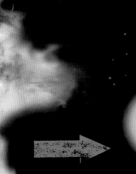

Protostar

Star birth nebula

Large star

Red giant

Planetary
nebula

White dwarf

Black dwarf

Black hole

Neutron star/ pulsar

Red supergiant star

Supernova
explosion

There are billions of stars in our galaxy, the Milky Way.

CHAPTER 5

Star Studies

Astronomers are scientists who study space and everything in it. By observing stars, astronomers have learned about a star's life in the universe, the future of our Sun, and the existence of other planets. Ancient astronomers had only their eyes to study and observe stars. Today, astronomers have more tools like giant telescopes that float in space!

 There are more stars in space than grains of sand on Earth's beaches and deserts.

Across the Universe

Unlike scientists who study life on Earth, astronomers can't watch a star's life from beginning to end. That would take billions of years. Instead, astronomers study stars of all different ages in space. By doing this, they will have a way to better understand the life cycles of stars.

The Hubble Space Telescope takes images of objects in space. It sends the information back to Earth for scientists to study.

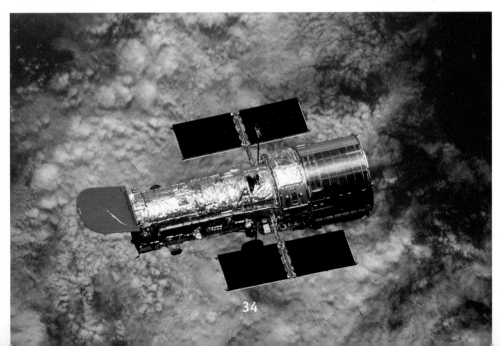

Our Sun is a yellow dwarf.

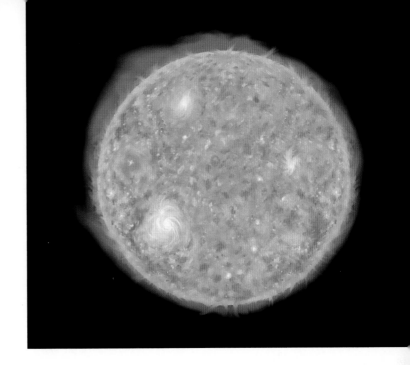

Our Closest Star

Scientists have learned a lot about stars by studying the Sun. While the Sun might seem special to us, it's a very ordinary, medium-sized star. Like other stars, the Sun sometimes violently erupts, sending out billions of tons of material into space. And, although it takes years for light from other stars to reach Earth, light from our Sun takes just over eight minutes to reach us.

The Sun's Future

Like all stars, the Sun will run out of fuel in its core one day. But that's not likely to happen for another five billion years! Once the Sun uses up all its hydrogen, it will grow up to 100 times bigger. When this happens, the red giant Sun will fill up Earth's sky and oceans will dry up.

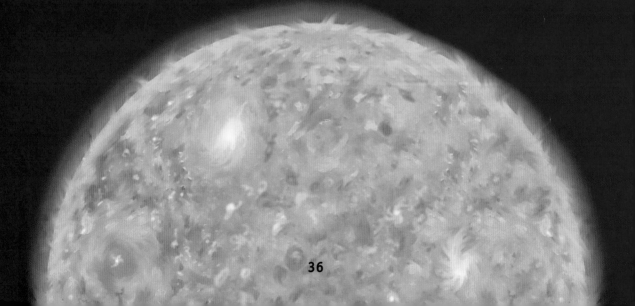

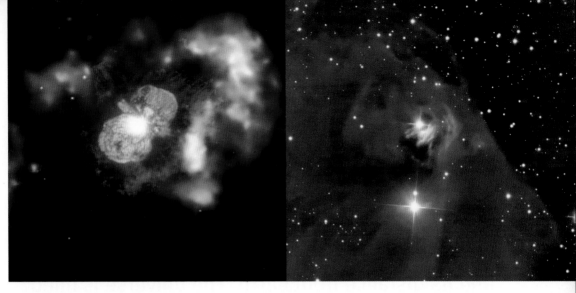

Eta Carina is a hot blue supergiant star that is losing gases.

The orange star in this image is T Tauri, a very young star.

Long Distance Light

With the exception of our Sun, all other stars are very far away from Earth, so astronomers must study their faint light to learn about them. From the light, astronomers can find out a star's age, size, and temperature. If the light from a distant star is blue, astronomers know that it's most likely a hot and large blue giant. If the light is red or orange, the star may be a cool dwarf or a giant star.

Chandra X-ray Observatory

Even though there are billions of stars, you can only see about 3,000 without telescopes or binoculars. Being able to see a star in the night sky depends on the amount of light it gives off and its distance from Earth. The universe is filled with stars that don't give off enough light or are too far away for us to see.

To help study some objects, astronomers use special space telescopes like the Chandra X-ray Observatory. Chandra can sense hot space objects, like stars, that give off X-rays. X-rays are a form of invisible energy that human eyes cannot see. Although a star may not seem bright to us, it is hot and sends out X-rays. Chandra can take special pictures of X-rays from different objects in space so that scientists can better understand what they look like.

This image of the Cat's Eye Nebula was formed from pictures taken by the Hubble Space Telescope and the Chandra X-ray Observatory. This planetary nebula shows a dying star. In a few million years the rest of the star will become a white dwarf.

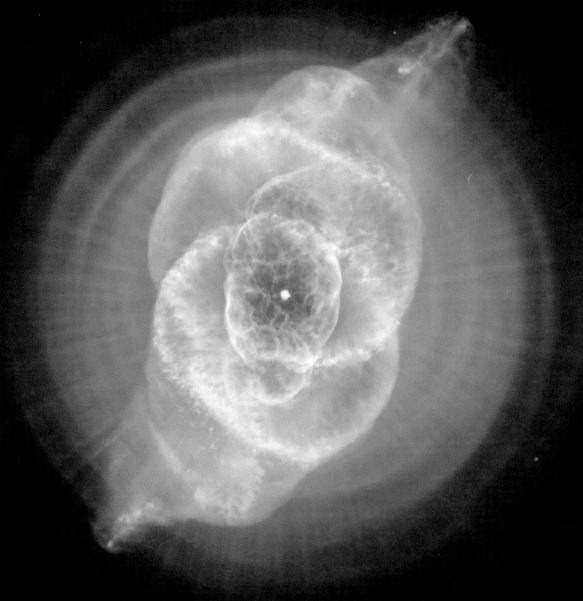

Other Planets, Other Worlds

Some young stars have rings of gas and dust spinning around them. These are leftovers from the nebula that formed the star. Over time, the rings of gas and dust can clump together to make planets, moons, and other space objects. Planets that travel around stars other than our Sun are called **exoplanets**.

Astronomers have discovered more than 330 exoplanets.

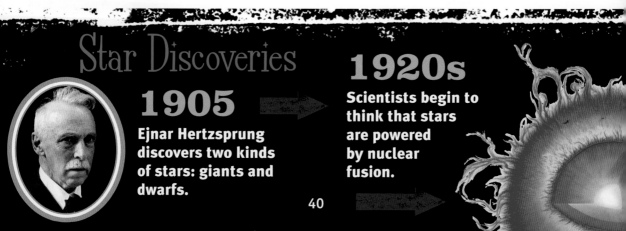

Star Discoveries

1905

Ejnar Hertzsprung discovers two kinds of stars: giants and dwarfs.

1920s

Scientists begin to think that stars are powered by nuclear fusion.

Changes in a star's brightness can tell astronomers if an exoplanet is circling a star. Some exoplanets travel in front of their parent stars and block out some of the star's light. This makes the star dimmer. Scientists can track this change in brightness and figure out if it's an exoplanet or something else causing the change.

In 1923, Edwin Hubble proved that the Milky Way is not the only galaxy in the universe.

1987

SN 1987A is discovered by scientists.

1995

A planet is discovered around another star for the first time.

Stars and Our Future

Experts have studied stars for centuries. While doing so, they have made some amazing discoveries, such as planets orbiting distant stars. For many years to come, those experts will continue to have questions and will look to billions of stars for answers.

G11.2-0.3 is a remnant of a supernova that scientists believe exploded in 386 C.E.

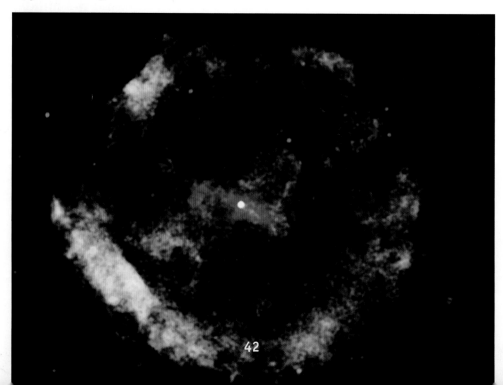

True Statistics

The speed of light: 186,000 mi. (300,000 km) per second

Number of stars in a galaxy: Billions

Number of galaxies in the universe: Billions and billions

Life span of our Sun: More than 10 billion years

Age of the universe: About 14 billion years

Percentage of stars that will become white dwarfs: About 99 percent

Time it takes for a white dwarf to become a black dwarf: Billions of years

Number of known exoplanets: More than 330

Did you find the truth?

F Stars live forever and never change at all.

T Stars are made from clouds of gas and dust called nebulae.

Resources

Books

Berger, Melvin, and Gilda Berger. *Do Stars Have Points?: Questions and Answers About Stars and Planets*. New York: Scholastic, 1998.

Chrismer, Melanie. *The Sun*. New York: Children's Press, 2005.

Driscoll, Michael. *A Child's Introduction to the Night Sky: The Story of the Stars, Planets, and Constellations, and How You Can Find Them in the Sky*. New York: Black Dog & Leventhal, 2004.

Galat, Joan Marie. *Dot to Dot in the Sky: Stories in the Stars*. North Vancouver, BC: Whitecap Books, 2002.

Hobson, Charles. *Seeing Stars*. San Francisco: Chronicle Books, 2001.

Simon, Seymour. *Stars*. New York: Smithsonian/HarperCollins Children's Books, 2006.

Wright, Kenneth. *Scholastic Atlas of Space*. New York: Scholastic, 2005.

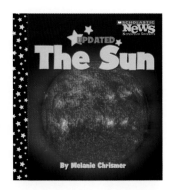

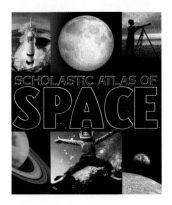

Organizations and Web Sites

World Book at NASA
www.nasa.gov/worldbook
Read articles about stars and other space objects.

Amazing Space
http://amazing-space.stsci.edu
Play games and learn about stars, telescopes, and more at this site created by the Space Telescope Science Institute.

Chandra X-ray Observatory Photo Album
www.chandra.harvard.edu/photo
View photographs taken by the Chandra X-ray Observatory.

Places to Visit

Rose Center for Earth and Space
American Museum of Natural History
Central Park W. at 79th St.
New York, NY 10024
(212) 769 5100
www.amnh.org/rose
Learn all about the history of the universe.

Griffith Observatory
2800 East Observatory Road
Los Angeles, CA 90027
(213) 473 0800
www.griffithobs.org
Watch the stars and meet other astronomy fans at this famous California observatory.

Important Words

black hole – a collapsed star with such strong gravity that light does not escape it

dwarfs – stars that are similar in size to our Sun

exoplanets – any planets traveling around stars that aren't our Sun

galaxies – systems containing millions or billions of stars

giants – stars that are tens of times larger than our Sun

gravity – a force that pulls two objects together

nebulae (NEH-byoo-lee) – giant clouds of gas and dust in space

neutron star – a very compact star that can remain after a supernova explosion

nuclear fusion (NOO-klee-ur FYOO-zhuhn) – a special kind of reaction that makes stars give off light

protostar – a ball of gas and dust in space that becomes a star after its core begins nuclear fusion

star clusters – groups of hundreds or thousands of stars bound together by gravity

supergiants – stars that are hundreds of times larger than our Sun

supernova – a powerful explosion that happens when very large stars die

Index

Page numbers in **bold** indicate illustrations

About the Author

Ker Than is a science writer living in New York City. He has a master's degree from New York University's Science, Health, and Environmental Reporting Program. Before becoming a freelancer, Ker was a staff writer at the science news Web sites LiveScience.com and Space.com, where he wrote about earthquakes, dinosaurs, black holes, and other interesting things.

PHOTOGRAPHS © 2008: Getty Images (p. 28; p. 39); iStockphoto (©Jim DeLillo, twinkling stars, p. 5; ©Manfred Konrad, p. 3; Martin Adams, p. 13; ©Mehmet Salih Guler, p. 9; ©George Argyropoulos, pp. 35–36; NASA (p. 34; CXC: Eureka Scientific, M. Roberts et al., p. 42, GSFC, M. Corcoran et al., Eta Carina, p. 37; ©Don Goldman, T Tauri, p. 37; ESA: A. Noriega-Crespo (SSC/Caltech), p. 12, A. Schaller, exoplanet, p. 41; Hubble Heritage (STScI/AURA), cover, J. Maiz Apellaniz (Inst. Astrofisica Andalucia) & Davide de Martin (skyfactory. org), p. 15; P. Challis & R. Kirshner, Harvard-Smithsonian Center for Astrophysics, and B. Sugerman, STScI, SN 1987A, p. 41, SOHO, back cover; JPL-Caltech: p. 12, p. 29, J. Hora (Harvard-Smithsonian CfA), p. 20, P.S. Teixeira Center for Astrophysics, Stellar Snowflake Cluster, p. 5; T. Pyle/ SSC, exoplanet, p. 40); Photodisc (p. 14); Photolibrary (p. 6; p. 10; p. 16; p. 23; pp. 25–26; p. 32; Ejnar Hertzsprung, p. 40; p. Edwin Hubble, p. 41); Tranz/Corbis (p. 27)